CH00747648

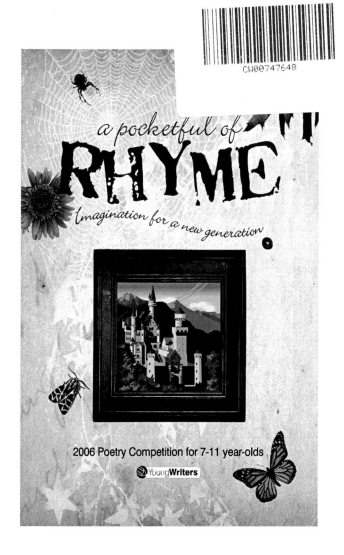

a pocketful of
RHYME
Imagination for a new generation

2006 Poetry Competition for 7-11 year-olds

YoungWriters

Verses From The North
Edited by Lynsey Hawkins

 Young**Writers**

First published in Great Britain in 2007 by:
Young Writers
Remus House
Coltsfoot Drive
Peterborough
PE2 9JX
Telephone: 01733 890066
Website: www.youngwriters.co.uk

All Rights Reserved

© Copyright Contributors 2007

SB ISBN 978-1 84602 780 2

Foreword

Young Writers was established in 1991 and has been passionately devoted to the promotion of reading and writing in children and young adults ever since. The quest continues today. Young Writers remains as committed to the nurturing of poetic and literary talent as ever.

This year's Young Writers competition has proven as vibrant and dynamic as ever and we are delighted to present a showcase of the best poetry from across the UK and in some cases overseas. Each poem has been selected from a wealth of *A Pocketful Of Rhyme* entries before ultimately being published in this, our fourteenth primary school poetry series.

Once again, we have been supremely impressed by the overall quality of the entries we have received. The imagination, energy and creativity which has gone into each young writer's entry made choosing the poems a challenging and often difficult but ultimately hugely rewarding task - the general high standard of the work submitted ensured this opportunity to bring their poetry to a larger appreciative audience.

We sincerely hope you are pleased with this final collection and that you will enjoy *A Pocketful Of Rhyme Verses From The North* for many years to come.

Contents

Cambois First School, Blyth

Alex Walker (7)	57
Katie Robinson (9)	57
Alice Smith (7)	57
Shane Gray (7)	58
Jordan Campbell (8)	58
Grant Walker (9)	59
Carl Calumboski (8)	59
Rhiannon Carr (8)	60
Lewis Gray (8)	60

John F Kennedy Primary School, Washington

Andrew MacKnight (10)	61
Christopher Leybourne (10)	61
Francesca Hall (10)	62
Francesca Cotton (10)	62
Jack Short (10)	63
Daniel Hylands (11)	63
Rebecca Hoseason (10)	64
Amy Williamson (10)	64
Callum Rutter (10)	64
Kate Robson (10)	65
Rebecca Eleanor Oliver (10)	65
Jack Spalding (10)	65
Charlotte Jane Casey (10)	66
Alexandra Heather Mitchell (10)	66
Sophie Henderson (10)	67
Daryl McMahon (10)	67
Kyle Taylor (11)	67
James Wilson (10)	68
Loren Toni Fernyhough (10)	68
Yasmin Corrigan (10)	68
Courtney Spencer (10)	69
Ben Robson (10)	69
William Edward Brightman (10)	69
Courtney Barnetson (10)	70
Jordan Watts (10)	70
Brandon Harkess (10)	70
Sophie Danskin (11)	71
Gavin Milroy (10)	71
Sarah Sweeney (10)	71

Charlotte Lesley McIntosh (11)   72
Emma Povey (10)   72
Emily Turnock Anderson (10)   73
Stephen Gettings (10)   73
Dean Farley (10)   74
Craig William Foster (10)   75
Anthony Lawson (10)   76
Adam Docherty   76
James Jackson (10)   77
Lucy McMahon (10)   77
Faye Chenery (10)   78
Emma Boxer (10)   79
Rachel Williams (10)   80
Brandon Black (10)   80

Red House School, Stockton-on-Tees

Benjamin Hunter (9)   81
Elliott Gibbons (9)   81
Holly Featherstone (9)   82
Theron Darlow (9)   82
Animesh Anand (9)   83
Stephen Blease (9)   83
Jacob Darlow (9)   84
Jessica Bedi (9)   84
Katrina Wright (9)   85
George Baker (9)   85
Alex Stephenson (9)   86
Christine Saltikov (9)   86
Harry Tomlinson (9)   86
Nanditha Pradeep (9)   87
Robert Morgan (9)   87
Sam James Dixon (9)   87
Olivia Crewe (9)   88
Scarlett Reeves (9)   88
Samantha Mason (9)   89
Erin Fleming (10)   89
Grace Hughes (10)   90
Joe Musgrave (9)   90
George Wall (9)   91
Megan Brineman (10)   91
Alexander Plahé (9)   92

Harry Bulmer (9)   92
Joseph Clarke (9)   93
Matthew Birch (9)   93
Sam Burchett (9)   94
Kane Hewson (10)   94
Josef Oliver Reilly (9)   95
Lewis Robinson (9)   95

St Bega's RC Primary School, Hartlepool
Rachael Burder (8)   95
Kristen Cambridge (10)   96
Phillipa Harrion (11)   96
Demi-Leigh Milburn (10)   97
Hayden Lynch (10)   97
Carl Young (9)   98
George Harrison (10)   98
Megan Lynch (10)   99
Robyn Hannon (9)   99
Dillon Johnson (10)   100
Daniel Robinson (9)   100
Amy Ridden (10)   100
Aidan Crawford (7)   101
Georgia Rochester (7)   101
Jack Purcell (7)   101
Devyn Olufemi Wood (9)   102
Alex Pringle-Arnell (8)   102
Lucy Lilley (10)   103
Katie Bradley (9)   103
Bethany Williams (7)   104
Emilee Pringle-Arnell (10)   104
Benjamin Dignen (8)   104
Atlanta Burgon (9)   105
Nathaniel Skidmore (8)   105
Patrick Burder (10)   105
Caitlin Lister (9)   106
Evie Robbins (8)   106
Emily Pettite (9)   107
Carl O'Sullivan (9)   107

The Poems

Bonfire

B onfires sparked, as lights flicker.
O n the bonfire, sparks hit the floor.
N ow we see the bright sparks of them all.
F lickers as I watch.
I t lights up the dark midnight sky.
R eady, waiting, I heard the biggest bang,
E nding the night with a spark.

Rebecca Butler (9)
Badger Hill Primary School, Saltburn by the Sea

Autumn Days

A utumn leaves drift and flutter to the ground,
U nderneath the leaves sleeps a
T ired baby hedgehog,
U pon the floor leaves are rotting,
M uddy leaves all over the floor,
N ude leaves swirling and twirling.

Hannah Garrett (9)
Badger Hill Primary School, Saltburn by the Sea

Autumn Days

The sun shines like a dim light,
A conker falls and cracks its shell,
The autumn leaves trickle down like umber hearts,
The bonfire is like a blazing lamp,
A whispering wind comes from the hills.

Lindsay Seccombe (9)
Badger Hill Primary School, Saltburn by the Sea

Bonfire Poem

B onfire flickers in the sky as the sun goes down.

O n the bonfire the logs crackle.

N ow it's time to wave and shout as the biggest

firework goes off.

F ire crackles on the floor,

I t lights up the dark, gloomy sky

R eady for the last flick in the bright sky and then *bang!*

E nd of the night.

Megan Scarff (9)
Badger Hill Primary School, Saltburn by the Sea

Always Having Dreams

A lways having dreams

U sing autumn wishes

T imes to remember

U sually enjoying Bonfire Night

M y friends all having fun

N ever being sad

T o go trick or treating

I am happy every day

M eeting new people

E very time is better than the last.

Adam Young (9)
Badger Hill Primary School, Saltburn by the Sea

Young Writers - A Pocketful Of Rhyme Verses From The North

It's Autumn

Leaves flutter in the misty autumn breeze,
Wild wind roars into the treetops,
The woods smell deeply of sweet autumn sap,
Old hay rattles in silence,
Burnt umber and scarlet leaves whistle from nowhere,
Leaves crackle as I drift through,
Conker trees fade into the distance,
As I flutter through the open air,
Nuts as hard as rocks,
A whirlwind of leaves and bark journey through
                                    the neighbourhood,
Autumn is here.

Georgia Eve Bint (9)
Badger Hill Primary School, Saltburn by the Sea

Autumn Time

Faded leaves gently fluttering down,
Russet and crimson leaves smelling musty,
Then crinkled and crackled on to the ground,
Faded leaves gently fluttering down.

Tick-tock, a pendulum swinging just like conkers,
Round polished and smooth conkers,
Glowing in the distance like a bell.
Tick-tock, a pendulum swinging just like conkers.

Hannah Clayton (9)
Badger Hill Primary School, Saltburn by the Sea

A Magical Poem

I wait restlessly in an immense cave
Like a dungeon,
Pitch-black, dim and dingy,
So far down
You can't hear anything.

I wait restlessly down in the potash
Like a wild dog,
So far down,
Vicious, insane and furious,
So far down you can't see anything.

I wait restlessly at the pit bottom
Like a transporter,
Towering and huge,
So far down
You can't feel anything.

Charlie Berry (8)
Badger Hill Primary School, Saltburn by the Sea

Autumn Leaves

The bonfire burns
As people dance,
Leopards leap from the fire,
The fluffy frost flies from the forest,
Children laugh and play,
The moonlight glows above the treetops,
Stars twinkle brightly in the distance.

Lauren Joyce (10)
Badger Hill Primary School, Saltburn by the Sea

I Was Alone In The Dark

I was alone in the dark,
The spooky house was scary.
Lights were flashing on and off.
A huge tarantula climbed its web
And I was scared of the tarantula
And there was a mouse on my foot.
It was cold as wind,
I was as cold as the wind.
I was screaming loudly.

Jethro Watson (8)
Badger Hill Primary School, Saltburn by the Sea

A Dark Night

The night is dark,
It's a midnight sky.
The sparkling moon reflects brightly
Making purple shadows,
Like ghosts.

The night is dark,
It's a windy sky.
The shining stars sparkle loudly,
Making grisly shapes
Like gremlins.

Sophie Hopper (8)
Badger Hill Primary School, Saltburn by the Sea

A Dark City

A dark city
Becoming darker,
As weird shadows pass.
It is like being down,
Deep down in the deserted mine.

A dark city
Becoming louder,
As British aeroplanes *boom!*
It is like an explosion
Deep down in the deserted mine.

A dark city
Becoming sinister,
As angry people shout.
It is like banging doors
Deep down in the deserted mine.

Jodie Clark (8)
Badger Hill Primary School, Saltburn by the Sea

Autumn

Autumn leaves swirl to the ground,
Damp smells whirl the burnt amber and brown leaves,
Autumn winds drift through the grass,
Leaves smell wet as I walk among them,
I can hear the break of a conker,
The leaves drop in the distance,
It is like autumn.

Abbie Summerson (9)
Badger Hill Primary School, Saltburn by the Sea

Alone In the Dark

Alone in a silent city,
Glowing lights follow me.
As the icy wind rustles through crumbled leaves,
Owls are hooting in my ears.

Alone in a mysterious city,
Winter trees are like arms reaching for me.
A full moon is shining brightly on my face,
Bats are silently waking up.

Alone in a deserted city,
Every step is heart-stopping.
Shadows twisting cruelly in every corner,
Cold rain is dripping from a rusty drainpipe.

Alone in a moonlit city,
Ancient gates are creaking.
Cats' eyes glowing wickedly, like fire,
In the distance dawn is rising.

Antonia Hetherington (8)
Badger Hill Primary School, Saltburn by the Sea

Darkness

Banging, screeching!
Rats running beside the crippled road.
Impossible to see anything.
Black shadows creeping,
In the dark city.

As night approaches,
Snapping twigs crack like bullets.
Impossible to escape.
Snapping your life,
In the dark city.

Thomas Samuel Lindley (8)
Badger Hill Primary School, Saltburn by the Sea

Darkness

A black cat walks on tattered walls,
Above a spiraling mass of darkness,
Enfolding a harsh and threatening landscape,
Dark is an icon of danger.

A vanishing figure blends into dim skies,
Strange shadows loom over an ashy path.
Weird things approaching in the pitch-black night,
Dark is an icon of danger.

Water softly flows near the banks of moonlit brooks,
Nature is waking, dawn is near,
Weird things chasing away,
Dark is an icon of danger.

Gabriel Walker (8)
Badger Hill Primary School, Saltburn by the Sea

Darkness

Outside, shadows moving slowly,
Dry amber leaves rustling loudly,
Voices echoing in the darkness,
Birds fluttering in the night's stillness.

Outside figures are creeping silently,
The moon shines brightly,
Hedgehogs crawling like babies,
Badgers sleeping.

Inside, above, people are dreaming,
Children twisting and turning,
Dreams about monsters,
Nightmares rushing through puzzled minds.

Inside down below I sit,
Waiting alone in the dark,
Everything is still,
Silence.

Molly Broughton (8)
Badger Hill Primary School, Saltburn by the Sea

First Day Down The Mine

Down the mine is full of rats and loud sounds,
Pit props snapping,
Roof collapsing,
Heavy stones falling.

Down the mine is scary, gloomy and dark,
I wish there was light.
I cannot see the silver moon.
I am in pain in the darkness.

Down the mine is pitch-black and very ghostly,
It's really frightening,
Sounds crashing,
It's creepy.

Down the mine is lonely,
It's really terrifying.
I shudder restlessly,
I have butterflies in my tummy.

Rebecca Clarkson (8)
Badger Hill Primary School, Saltburn by the Sea

The Darkness

A dark path,
No one around in the darkness,
But somewhere a kid is crying,
The silver moon is shining.
As darkness falls,
The noise is louder,
Then suddenly quieter and then silent,
Like a sleeping mouse.

A dark path,
No one around in the darkness,
Except a small spider in the corner,
Spinning a web,
It sparkles
In the silver moonlight.

James Bullock (8)
Badger Hill Primary School, Saltburn by the Sea

Darkness

In the dark things are creeping,
Fierce rats squealing, long-toothed cats crawling.
Dangerous people looming in darkness,
Savage and frightening.
A crescent moon shines through the darkness.

In the night bats are squealing,
Owls hooting,
Clocks chiming,
Moonless night falling into the darkness.

In the dark, shadowy and gloomy,
Suddenly stars sparkling through the night,
The moon shining brightly in the dark sky.

Christopher Fleming (8)
Badger Hill Primary School, Saltburn by the Sea

It's Like The End Of The World

Silent figures scurrying in the darkness,
Rich people hidden in closets.
Outside the sky is ghostly black,
Gruesome shadows upon the wall.
Bang! Bang! Bang!
Echoes the gun.
It's like the end of the world.

Royal windows smashing in the darkness,
Death-trapping doors creak.
Haunting cries groan,
Spirits rise and the dreams open.
Whoo! Whoo! Whoo!
Hoots the owl.
It's like the end of the world.

Jordan Edwards (8)
Badger Hill Primary School, Saltburn by the Sea

Darkness Passes

Rippling water reflects off a crescent moon.
Flowing water gathering stones,
Turning them into smooth pebbles.
Dark skies floating over a murky sea.
Fearful rocks tumbling.

Mountains craggy like rooftops,
Clouds twisting and turning.
Stars twinkling in the midnight sky.
Thunder crashes in the thick black stillness.
The world is cloaked in darkness.

Wild winds whirl.
A raging sea topples over jagged rocks.
Hard rain lashes down.
The wounded world is waiting.
Then dawn enfolds into a flood of light.

Ellen Payne (8)
Badger Hill Primary School, Saltburn by the Sea

Deep In The Darkness

You hear bats echo
Deep down in the mine.

Rats nibble my feet
Deep down in the mine.

I saw singing birds killed by the gas
Deep down in the mine.

I heard horses galloping
Deep down in the mine.

I wait patiently
Deep in the mine.

I sit in the darkness
Alone in the ironstone.

Zach North (8)
Badger Hill Primary School, Saltburn by the Sea

Slowly And Silently

Slowly and silently,
Over the lonely graveyard,
Like a baby in the darkness,
I heard eerie crying,
Wind moaning,
Night brooding.

Slowly and silently,
On the cracked bench,
Like a ghostly widow,
I saw a grim shadow,
Ghouls muttering,
Dawn looming.

Slowly and silently,
Under the warm earth wrapped
Like a blanket,
I heard spirits crying,
Time falling,
Dawn looming.

Katie Lowe (8)
Badger Hill Primary School, Saltburn by the Sea

The Dark

Day passes by
And I am alone.
Outside dark is descending.
Inside, dimly lit by lanterns,
I wait,
Shadows lurking,
Sinister sounds echoing.

Outside starless skies stroll.
Inside is pitch-black,
Shadows lurking,
Ultra silent, like a supersonic ray,
Confusing me.

Day passes by
And I am alone.
Outside the dark envelops,
Inside is a nightmare.
I wait, shadows lurking.
Candlelight fading away
As I ascend from the mine.

Elliott Hick (8)
Badger Hill Primary School, Saltburn by the Sea

Poem Of The Dark

The moon is shining brightly
But it's only a reflection,
Falling in darkness,
Goosebumps on top of goosebumps.

It's gloomy darkness,
Like a huge black cave.
It is a murky place,
Pitch-black darkness.

Inky black.
All alone and terrified.
Howls from the garden.
Dog barking from next door.

Adelle Oglesby (8)
Badger Hill Primary School, Saltburn by the Sea

Darkness

Miners are courageous,
Working deep in the darkness,
Blasting the ironstone,
Tipping into the tubs,
Pit props almost snapping,
Groaned in agony,
Beating hearts pound,
Shocking damage inside bodies,
Fearful ironstone crashing,
Jet-black down the mine.

Miners suffocating in savage gas,
Lost deep in the darkness,
Miners choking and spluttering,
Slowly they hit the dirt,
Red eyes swelling,
Last thoughts of the upper world.

Jason Parry (8)
Badger Hill Primary School, Saltburn by the Sea

In The Dark

Bats swooping in never-ending tunnels,
Pitch-black stillness,
Things moving inside in the dark,
Inky-black shadows watch fiercely
Against the filthy walls,
Like coal.

A rumbling storm overhead,
The wind is really strong,
Blowing angrily outside in the dark,
Purple clouds crash loudly
Against thunder,
Like fire.

Mary Fletcher (8)
Badger Hill Primary School, Saltburn by the Sea

The Darkness

The dark is full of people stealing.
It is very gloomy and mysterious.
Full of black cats and horrifying shadows.
The dark is full of restless rats.

The woods are alive
With wolves hunting and owls hooting.
The glistening moon shines softly
Off the nearest puddle.
Stalking eyes looking for the kill.

Ghostly trains crashing in the darkness.
Wounded people screaming and wailing.
The scariest place on mysterious Earth,
The dark, when you are alone.

Kane Fickling (8)
Badger Hill Primary School, Saltburn by the Sea

Darkness Poem

I sat alone in darkness,
All around silent shadows watching,
Dark water trickling down stone walls,
Bats flapping above my skull,
Calling, deep in the dark.

Cold, damp,
Silent on my own.
Pit ponies' hooves *clip-clop*,
Driver boys laughing
And calling deep in the dark.

Mine horses wanting to be in sunshine.
I want to be in sunshine.
I am worried about the explosion,
I feel like I am going to die,
Deep in the dark.

Lewis Treloar (8)
Badger Hill Primary School, Saltburn by the Sea

The Dark

It was as dark as dark could be, not a thing to see,
Trickling water gliding down rough rocks,
Plop, plop, plop.
Dusty grains drifting up my nose,
I could not see a thing,
Screeching, nibbling hairy brown rats,
Shivering shoulders
As cold as ice,
Quickly I dashed to the light,
Everything turned back to normal.

Scott Tait (8)
Badger Hill Primary School, Saltburn by the Sea

Dark In The City

The night is full of car engines rumbling,
Shadowy footsteps passing.
The glimmering moon shines brightly
On the night singing birds.
Badgers silently creeping
Into the cosy burrows.
Cold babies crying.

The night is full of owls hunting,
Hungry cats creeping.
The shining, starry moon
Shines brightly on the night
Scuttling badgers.
Creepy sounds making animals scatter.
People feeling like they're underground,
Cats hunting for food.
People dreaming of dark water under the stormy sea.

Aaron Mann (8)
Badger Hill Primary School, Saltburn by the Sea

Darkness

The dark is full of hooting owls,
Shadows lurking in the darkness,
Gloomy eyes looking for prey,
Spooky shapes moving inconspicuously.

Craggy hills cracking like mud,
Rivers drifting silently,
Rats scurrying speedily,
Ships hurrying on the fierce sea.

Dreams flying around me,
The moon is turning the Earth,
As nasty nightmares float,
Good dreams are hovering in minds.

Louis Winspear (8)
Badger Hill Primary School, Saltburn by the Sea

The Moon Shines Brightly

The dark is full of things screeching,
Dogs howling, rats squeaking and nibbling,
Cats wailing and calling.
In the woods owls hooting, moles rooting,
Foxes hunting for rabbits and rabbits digging for carrots.

Mysterious people looking for trouble
In the dingy darkness.
Noises everywhere and creeping, sneaking figures.

Somebody woke up the black crows.
A scream let out across the night,
Made me quiver to the bone.
The sharpie dog snapped and growled,
As I crossed the bridge.

The moon glows like fire, shining silver.
Stars twinkling in the sky.
Nothing to hear at all.
Silently sleeping.

Charlie Powell (8)
Badger Hill Primary School, Saltburn by the Sea

Happiness

Happiness is like sucking a chewy sweet,
It's like there's a crazy party in your mouth,
Wonderful Christmas Day, you see the great presents
And they try to hug you tight.
You go to a fantastic theme park
And the racing roller coaster drags you like crazy.
Going on a wonderful holiday,
Where the warm swimming pool has loads of colourful fish.

Connor Buckley (10)
Benedict Biscop CE Primary School, Moorside

Running Home As The Clock Strikes Twelve

The trembling of great fear,
As it ripples around your soul.
The howling of the cruel wind
When it wriggles straight into your heart,
Shadows flicker as they follow you home.
The roar of mighty thunder
As it crumbles all hope like a merciless lion
Pouncing on its prey!
Self-conscious laughing
As it scrambles your mind in the heart of the night.
Now your powerful determination will show you the route home . . .

Ryan Enguita (10)
Benedict Biscop CE Primary School, Moorside

The Warm Bed

The pitter-patter of the rain
As it bangs anxiously on your roof and then suddenly stops.
When the gloomy darkness looks over your room
And blinds you like pepper spray.
The only things that keep you warm are your bed
Which holds you like an elephant protecting its young
And the snugly quilt that wraps around you tightly
Like a snake catching its terrified prey.
Then to your relief the light creeps in slowly
And fights the darkness away.
Finally the alarm clock screams,
'Get up, get up, it's the start of another day.'

Jonathan Young (10)
Benedict Biscop CE Primary School, Moorside

Midnight Is Peace

Sky turns dark,
Moon appearing,
Shining brightly
Like beams of light.
Glistening stars
Shimmering sweetly,
As pure wisdom surrounds,
Flowing gently.

Crawling bugs
Scattered on the ground,
While howling wolves
Walk swiftly forward.
Hooting owls
Soaring through the night,
Whilst wonders of peace
Spread wildly.
Wind swaying
To and fro,
With tall green trees rustling.
Darkness goes bright,
And playful children awake.
The sun rises,
It's the start of a new day!

Skye Golledge (10)
Benedict Biscop CE Primary School, Moorside

The Perfect Home For Nightmares (My Head!)

After watching scary films you know you shouldn't have seen,
Do be warned they will not give you lovely, friendly dreams.
The sky is getting darker
And clouds are filling up the air,
The darkness creeping up on you,
Like a very creepy bear.
Your heart starts pounding wildly,
As if you're going to explode,
Just like standing right in the middle
Of a very busy road.
The sound of a clashing prison door,
As thunder gets locked up once more,
For murdering the friendly twins Hope and Faith,
But he won't do it anymore!
Then sadness starts mocking you again and again,
And then there comes the pain.
The wind is howling outrageously,
As it races through the streets,
And then it starts to numb both of your tiny little feet.
All things good have now disappeared,
Which makes things really weird.
Your hope is soaring out of your soul,
And off to another world.

Emily Cummings (11)
Benedict Biscop CE Primary School, Moorside

Midnight

The flowing of absolute darkness
As it creeps up on you like a howling ghost.
The crashing and splashing of rain
As it falls at your feet.
The banging of the thunder
As it abuses the lightning with its bold, brass voice.
The striking of the lightning,
When it glows with anger and howls an evil cackle.
The ferocious wind wrapping around your trembling feet
So you can no longer move.
The whimpering of your terrified soul
As it shakes with fear as the darkness creeps up on you.
The smirking of fear
Attacking your soul as it races wildly down your spine
And swirls all around you.
The grandfather clock which towers over the room
As it ticks and chimes when the hand strikes twelve
And the pendulum sways and sings his song once more.
The laughing of trees with their moaning and groaning
As their wicked faces howl at your stunned face.
The creaking and slamming of the old, oak doors
Like thunderbolts as they shout at each other.
The clashing of the old wooden windows
As they gossip away like two old ladies.
The sobbing of hope
As it leaks out of your sorrowful soul like water in a tap,
This is midnight and I am scared.

Samantha J Clark (10)
Benedict Biscop CE Primary School, Moorside

The Sound Collector

(Inspired by 'The Sound Collector' by Roger McGough)

A woman called this morning
Dressed all in pink and white
Put every sound into her purse
And carried them to the light.

The barking of my dog
The laughing of my mum
The shouting of my dad
And the laughing of the sun.

The screaming of a baby
The munching of my neighbour
The beeping of a car
And a teenager in labour.

The smacking of the ground
The talking of my sister
The humming of a bee
And the writing of a lister.

The ticking of a clock
The scratching of a lion
The swishing of a curtain
And the brother of a liar.

The panting of my heart
The squeaking of a mouse
The creaking of a stair
A little hole in my house.

A woman called this morning
Dressed in pink and white
Put every sound in her purse
And carried them to the light.

Kaitlin Common (9)
Benedict Biscop CE Primary School, Moorside

Through The Forest

The howling of the ferocious wind,
Twisting and turning through the forest towards you.
The blackness of the sky
Attacking you like an angered tiger
Which has been starved for weeks on end.
The squelching of the ravenous mud,
Swallowing you up violently.
The abuse of fear,
Sitting in your crumbling soul,
Besieging your disappearing hope.
There's a rustling in the bushes
And your heart stops as you turn to find . . .

Mark Chapman (10)
Benedict Biscop CE Primary School, Moorside

Love

Love is red like a blazing sun in the sparkling sky.
Singing birds in the blossom trees,
Sounds like peaceful music which makes me feel happy.
Delicious dark chocolate melts in my throat
And slithers down to my tummy.
Beautiful flowers grow all around my house
And the scent drifts through the open window.
Love feels like a great hug
And it makes you feel happy.

Sarah Casey (10)
Benedict Biscop CE Primary School, Moorside

Haunted House

The rattling keys ticking as the wind rushes quickly by
Heart beating I get extremely scared
Dogs howling as the rain hits the kennel
Street lights flickering like lightning
As the wind rocks it from side to side
Owl hooting as it swoops down and hunts its prey
Wind racing madly round the empty, cold street
Hailstones bouncing as the lightning strikes
Heating ticking as it heats up the freezing room.

Michael Carr (10)
Benedict Biscop CE Primary School, Moorside

Hate

Hate is black because in the gloomy, empty streets
There are no lights.
From the distance a dreadful scream comes
And explodes in my ears.
The soggy, mouldy bread melting in my mouth
Tastes like a drop of petrol on my tongue.
A disgusting smell goes up my nose every two minutes
As a garbage truck passes my house.

Brad Blakelock (10)
Benedict Biscop CE Primary School, Moorside

Nerves Building

All alone in the dark,
In your body there is a feeling,
A horrible, dark, miserable feeling.
You turn around in hope that someone will be there,
Your pounding heart is in your mouth as there is nobody in sight,
Apart from the smallest owl tooting like a flute.

As you slowly walk on there is something in your soul,
Boom, boom, boom
It bashes and pushes trying desperately to break free.
It cries and cries but nobody can help.
This feeling grows and grows, swallowing you whole
And you can not turn to anyone, not even yourself anymore.

Butterflies swooping and twirling inside your stomach,
This might sound nice, but it is not at all.
It attacks and sets out to destroy your soul,
You feel like screaming but your mouth will not move.
It becomes worse and worse - up, down, side, side,
Then suddenly it stops as you reach your house,
It is nice and still your nerves have settled.

Elizabeth Quinn (10)
Benedict Biscop CE Primary School, Moorside

Light Coming

My life is sprinting away from me
As a mouse from a ravenous cat.
Death is coming like a bird for a warm.
Soul abandoning because there is no hope now.
Hope extinguished as a fire would be.
Joy given up like the coward it is.
Light drawing near, I think my time is almost gone . . .

Niall O'Brien-Bird (10)
Benedict Biscop CE Primary School, Moorside

Horror

The howling of the wind
As it races widely round the dark, empty street.
The laughing of the ghost
As it echoes all around.
The shadow of darkness
Which covers your dark, cold room.
The tapping of trees
That climb up your solid walls.
The cawing of birds
As they swoop quickly past your window.
The fading of items
As they disappear slowly in the darkness.
The creaking of stairs
That scare you to *sleep!*

Matthew Prest (10)
Benedict Biscop CE Primary School, Moorside

Hope

Hope is yellow like the blazing sun,
in the magnificent sky.

Hope smells like fresh grass cuttings
that is coming from the farmers' fields.

In the trees birds sing a new song
as if a new year had started.

Hope tastes like toasted buns with butter on it
because it gives me a warm feeling.

Hope feels like training and training
for the Grand National.

Christopher Morton (10)
Benedict Biscop CE Primary School, Moorside

Scared

The sky is crying loudly
As the thunder and lightning screech as they clash
Like a vicious cat chasing an innocent mouse.
The joyful warmth inside you is dying,
When you run across the shaking floor
The darkness lies and laughs at you.
The wind is howling wildly
Like a werewolf at midnight when there is a full moon.
The trees are transforming into death-eating ghosts,
Now you are trembling rapidly
As fear chases you
Through this empty, gloomy night!

Jane Jobling (10)
Benedict Biscop CE Primary School, Moorside

Life's Path

Life is like a railway,
Its path is yet unknown.
It goes through many dark tunnels
And brightly coloured plains,
Places full of hope and love
And others with depression and deceit
Until you and your forthcoming fate come to meet.
Suddenly a gust of icy wind speeds
Along your life's long path,
Dragging you along the track,
You cannot head back.

Tom Langley (10)
Benedict Biscop CE Primary School, Moorside

The Confusion Of Sound!

The tapping of an oak tree at your window,
Like a murderer climbing up the rickety drainpipe,
The crying of a baby next door,
Like a moping zombie behind the solid wall.
The fear of death as it grows in your mind,
The dripping of icy water from your drains,
Like a clock ticking slowly at the back of your brain,
At this moment in time you're sinking deeper into your bed,
So much going on inside your confused head,
Right now your hope is fading away,
Will you ever see your hope again?
But are these sounds just an illusion
In this mind of total confusion?

James Irwing (10)
Benedict Biscop CE Primary School, Moorside

Dreams

The tweeting of small birds
As they sing great tunes.
The rushing of joy
As it wanders straight past you.
The waving of trees
As you lean against them.
The brightness of the sun
As it beats down blinding you.
The sailing of the peaceful blue sky
When it looks so empty.
The ripples of the flowers
As they smile at everyone going past.

Megan Innes (10)
Benedict Biscop CE Primary School, Moorside

Spooky Haunted House

As you walk up to the haunted house,
The wind is rustling madly.
The sky is very dark and creepy,
As you walk to the wooden door.
When you open the door,
You see straight away paintings with googly eyes
And bloody mouths.
As you walk down the creepy corridor,
You can see soldiers standing violently.
As you look through the broken window
You can see the rain falling rapidly
And the spooky cemetery with old gloomy gravestones.
When you walk out of the haunted house
You can hear owls and wolves which make you scared.

Stephen McGuire (10)
Benedict Biscop CE Primary School, Moorside

Hope

The moving of hope when it creeps towards you
A dove flying gracefully as it flies across a calm, golden sun
Excitement bubbling in my mind
A soft pillow when I lay my head down at night
A glimmer of light to show you where to go
Angels beautifully singing while flowers are blooming rapidly
A bee racing round an oak tree
The soft sun rising on a brand new day.

Jessica Hall (10)
Benedict Biscop CE Primary School, Moorside

Happiness

As you get up out of bed
Joy starts celebrating like a wedding.
The rising sun happily comes up
And starts shining through.
While you have your cooked breakfast
Love starts jumping wildly and knocking at your door
Like a very excited young child.
As you get your clothes on
Hope is wondering what good things are going to happen.
When you are playing the time stops
Because the fun is taking over.
Lasting for ages the day seems it's stopped
Like a watch which freezes.

Ian Wright (10)
Benedict Biscop CE Primary School, Moorside

Sparkling Snow

The smooth, sparkling snow
Is falling outside,
It's coming up to Christmas,
What a surprise!

I'm wrapping up pressies
And I'm full of glee,
All for my family
Under the tree!

M-m-m-milk and cookies
All for me,
I'm write a note
Just for Lee!

Gabrielle Middlewood (9)
Benedict Biscop CE Primary School, Moorside

The Sound Collector

(Inspired by 'The Sound Collector' by Roger McGough)

A lion called this morning
Dressed in blue PJs
He put every sound into a sack
And carried them all over town.

The screaming of the school kids
The shouting of the teachers
The banging of the hammer
The rustling of the leaves.

The munching of the hippo
The roaring of the lion
The charging of the river
The buzzing of the bee.

The splashing of the fish
The flapping of the bird
When the elephant squirts its water
The chewing of the giraffe
And when the sound collector
Finished his work he had a sack full of sound.

Cameron Chandler (9)
Benedict Biscop CE Primary School, Moorside

Rain

Eyes peering from windows
Babies crying like hyenas laughing
Children going crazy
Because they can't go outside
Children going bananas
Old grannies in their wet boots.

Declan Gooch (8)
Benedict Biscop CE Primary School, Moorside

The Sound Collector

(Inspired by 'The Sound Collector' by Roger McGough)

A lion called this morning
Dressed in black and grey
Put every sound into a bag
And carried them away.

The scratching of a lion
The buzzing of a bee
The splashing of water
The rustling of a tree.

The buzzing of a bee
The slapping of a knee
The rustling of the trees
The rustling of the leaves.

Josh Peart (10)
Benedict Biscop CE Primary School, Moorside

The Puppy

Little puppy
Thy sunny day
My lovely cuddle
Now come to play!

Am I
Growing
Or are you shrinking?
I don't know please tell me.

For I jump,
And play.
So let's go out
Another day.

Alex Lewis King (9)
Benedict Biscop CE Primary School, Moorside

A World Of Excitement

It's fun, it's wondrous, it's great and thunderous.
There are turtles and mares and horses and hares.
It's fun, it's wondrous, it's great and thunderous.
There are lollies and sweets and great chocolate treats.
It's fun, it's wondrous, it's great and thunderous.
There are birds and bees in big green trees.
It's fun, it's wondrous, it's great and thunderous.
There are games like chess which can make a huge mess.
It's fun, it's wondrous, it's great and thunderous.
There's grass and there are seas and different countries.
It's fun, it's wondrous, it's great and thunderous.
There are monkeys and bears in great big chairs.
It's fun, it's wondrous, it's great and thunderous.
There's sun in the morning and the moon in the night.
What else in the world will make you excite?

Luca Cassidy-Irvine (9)
Benedict Biscop CE Primary School, Moorside

Thunder

Thunder crashing
Children hiding
Babies crying
Dogs howling
Cats hiding
Dark clouds in the sky
Trees falling down and down
Power going off
At night candles lighting up houses
People moaning when they are tired
People going back to sleep
Finally the thunderstorm's over
And everyone is back to sleep.

Adam Stewart (8)
Benedict Biscop CE Primary School, Moorside

A Playful Dog

Little dog,
Thy autumn's play,
You run around
And bark all day.

I make a vow
To play with you,
As well as playing
With other animals too.

For all you catch
And play with a ball,
You always come
When I start to call.

Your day is coming to the end,
You go and start to rest.
Your bed is soft and comfy
And is just the best.

There you are in your bed,
Looking so cute,
You wriggle and wriggle
Then everything turns to mute.

Kate Robson (9)
Benedict Biscop CE Primary School, Moorside

Rain

Rain clashing to the ground
and making very big puddles.
Children splashing and sloshing
and making their boots wet.
Children splashing and screaming
and having fun.
Finally the rain has stopped.

Teagan Brown (8)
Benedict Biscop CE Primary School, Moorside

Sounds In The Playground

I hear all the sounds in every playground
And in every park,
Today I visit a playground.

The sound of children goes like this . . .
Shout
Scream
Leap,
Pop,
And
Hop.

The sound of the teachers goes like this . . .
Blow it,
Stop it,
Shout it,
Scream it.

Now I left it like this . . .
No sound at all,
Now that's how it should be,
Now no teacher can complain about that,
Can they?

Hannah Freeman (9)
Benedict Biscop CE Primary School, Moorside

Rain

Soon as it stars to rain
Children start to pull on their wellies
Small children splashing in puddles
People shivering in the wet weather
The rain falls down like crystals
As it hits the ground it sounds
Like thousands of ping-pong balls hitting the ground
Eventually the sun comes out
And leaves a rainbow in the sky.

Alexandra Anderson (8)
Benedict Biscop CE Primary School, Moorside

Snow

Birds are huddling up in a tree
Sledges are slipping and sliding down a hill
Children tucked up to keep them warm
Dogs are stuck in a slushy, mushy mess
Children are anxious to get out to play
Dads are furious because their car won't move
Hot chocolate bubbling in a cup
Happy children racing down a hill
Lots of snowflakes falling to the ground
Snow has gone
Children are in after a busy day in the snow.

Rehanna Hayes (9)
Benedict Biscop CE Primary School, Moorside

Fear

Fear is black like flashing
lightning in a storm.

Fear tastes like cold lobster
in the cold sea.

It smells like a cigarette
and an ashtray.

It looks like a dark
abandoned home.

It sounds like fingernails
scratching a chalkboard.

It feels like seaweed in a rock pool
on the seashore.

Lewis Charlton Leonard (9)
Benedict Biscop CE Primary School, Moorside

One Winter's Day

One winter's day, the snow was falling,
The small creatures would be crawling.
The little children would be snowballing,
Some children were wanted because their mums
                                        were calling.

The children were screaming,
The light were beaming.
They'd just been dreaming,
They were still tired but still admired.

Markus Cassidy-Irvine (9)
Benedict Biscop CE Primary School, Moorside

The Sound Collector

(Based on 'The Sound Collector' by Roger McGough)

'A stranger called this morning
Dressed all in black and grey
Put every sound into a bag
And carried them away.'

The laughing of the children
The barking of the dog
The tweeting of the bird
And the movement of the log.

The crackling of the fire
The whistling of the wind
The turning of the handle
And the rubbish getting binned.

The chatting of the ladies
The cheering of the lads
The buzzing of the bees
And the shouting of the dads.

Charlotte Oxley (9)
Benedict Biscop CE Primary School, Moorside

Love

Love is red like a thumping heart beating
It tastes like hot runny pudding melting in the sun
It smells like a freshly baked cake coming out of the oven
It looks like two tweeting birds flying through the trees
It sounds like the blooming flowers growing tall in the breeze
It feels like warmth inside you coming close to your heart
You feel like smiling when you feel it
You laugh with your friends
You prance all around
You can't stop feeling happy
You want to give more and more
Love is something special that's one thing for sure.

Abigail Chandler (9)
Benedict Biscop CE Primary School, Moorside

Anger

Anger is as black as a night with no moon,
It sounds like bats screeching out of tune.

Anger is like a belt being tightened round your waist,
Bitter lemon is its hateful taste.

Fist clenched, teeth gritted,
I threw a bench where someone was seated.

You really try to stop crying,
You are so angry you have to keep trying.

You have to keep it cool,
But really anger is a bit of a fool!

Evelyn Earl (9)
Benedict Biscop CE Primary School, Moorside

Love

The colours blue and pink make the word love,
Fly so high like the birds above.
The birds a-chirping up in the air
While I sit here gazing up there.
It smells like nature's perfume,
Looks like a pink and blue flower growing.
Finally the sun is going
And I am lying here on the hay,
That's enough love for today.

Lauren Briggs (9)
Benedict Biscop CE Primary School, Moorside

Little Bee

Little bee
Thy summer's day
My thoughtless mind
Has washed away.

Am I like a bee
Or not?
Or am I just a boy
Like Scott?

For me and my bee
We live happily
For we dance and prance
And fall into a trance.

Though your days are coming to a rest
And we have been the best of friends
I really liked our days together
And I'll miss you forever and ever.

Luke Millward (9)
Benedict Biscop CE Primary School, Moorside

Eagle

As I spotted an eagle soaring as it swerved,
Little did I know I was embracing hope,
It distinguished malice and let me relinquish hatred,
Happiness enlightened me and through my blood
                                courage curved.

As the eagle ducked into a dive
I felt joy but then it sank,
I thought I was going to be sick,
As the eagle didn't see the rock and thought it would die.

Suddenly it turned and dodged the rock,
My heart leapt for joy.
The eagle returned
And out from my body sorrow was awkwardly locked.

Sean Nicholson (10)
Benedict Biscop CE Primary School, Moorside

Sadness

Sadness is dark blue because it is like
the dark night covering the whole empty town.
When the dark night comes,
the only thing you can hear is sad people crying.
The taste of the soggy sprouts makes me feel really sad
as they dribble down my throat.
As the dark night comes you can smell burning petrol
and wood from a ghastly fire coming from the homeless people.
Although the dark night is over and the morning is coming
you don't feel like getting up.

Kieran Ward (10)
Benedict Biscop CE Primary School, Moorside

Walking Home

Dogs are crouching in the garden,
Barking rapidly like a thunderstorm steaming.
Hope is escaping through the deadly heart
Like a volcano rushing down the crumbling mountains.
Fear is building through the soul,
As it builds an unstoppable wall.
The sound of thunder and lightning
When it screams and shouts.
The shaking of the bushes,
As the rain thrashes on the ground.
Owls hooting in the air repeatedly
While bins crash ferociously.
Home is standing in the distance,
Tears are trickling down your face,
Who knows what lies ahead?
You're frantically wishing you were in bed.

Joseph Steel (10)
Benedict Biscop CE Primary School, Moorside

Midnight

As midnight strikes
The ancient (but shining) bells in the steeple
Chatter noisily amongst themselves
Birds sing a sweet song
For the welcoming of a new day
Gloom races rapidly around the city
Like an uncontrollable car
But doesn't hide the beautiful stars
Gleaming in the night sky
The dawn breaks
And hours move on
Soon it is night-time
Everyone sleeps
While they wait for a new day to come.

Lauren Ross (10)
Benedict Biscop CE Primary School, Moorside

Love

Love is red like a gleaming love heart.
It tastes like warm chocolate pudding that melts in your mouth.
It smells like a hot cookie just getting cooked.
It looks like the beaming red-hot sun.
It sounds like the waves just coming on the shore.
It feels like a warm feeling inside
Like when you have just fallen in love.
Love is everywhere if you just go and find it.

Lauren Sampson (9)
Benedict Biscop CE Primary School, Moorside

The Greatness Of Life

Life is like a conundrum,
It runs through your blood,
Flowing to your brain
Not knowing what to do.
Your heart is like a blazing fire,
Shining through when you're scared.
The overwhelming hope
Breaking down all your fear.
Elderly spirits watching over you,
Just checking you're alright.
Friendship flies through your window,
As it's like a bird which never stops.
New life is like the golden sunshine
Filling you with great cheer,
So I would make the most of it,
Just while you can.
You will always feel love,
As it wraps round you like a snug blanket,
To keep you warm when you're cold at night.

Luke Russell (10)
Benedict Biscop CE Primary School, Moorside

The Lovely Weekend

The weekend when the sun always smiles
Like a Cheshire cat smiles at a mouse.
When I am on my bike
It screeches madly with fear
As I go over the massive mud jumpers!
The joy is jumping
Like someone who has just won ten million pounds!
The soft black leather couch was cuddling you
As you sink into its massive cushiony black arms.
White smooth high tech PSP is playing
With its smooth, black, rounded volume control
Like a baby with its rattle!

Callum Riddell (11)
Benedict Biscop CE Primary School, Moorside

Love Is All Around

Love is everywhere
In houses and streets
Twirling round and round
Like a whirlpool in the sea.

Everyone is happy
Skipping round the park
Everyone has somebody
To make their life complete.

It tastes like a mix of candy
From the sweet shop
That is more tender
Than a lollipop.

It smells like a rose
Starting to open
What is better than
A love emotion?

Emma Jayne Davison (9)
Benedict Biscop CE Primary School, Moorside

The Shadow

A shadow sails through the murky dimness
Of your deserted cellar and hall
And who can tell what he's discovering,
Howling with the echoes of speeding bangs.
'It can't be a ghost,' you say to yourself,
Glancing over the windowpane,
But the universe outside is muted and tranquil.

As the shadow sails outside,
A shadow sailing fills the room
And filters through your open door.
'It can't be a ghost,' you say to yourself.
Traveling outside to turn out the lamp,
But the passageway is as black as night!

Katie Walton (9)
Benedict Biscop CE Primary School, Moorside

Anger

Anger is red lava trickling down a volcano.
It tastes like a bin of chilli sauce getting shoved in your mouth.
It smells smoky and hot, like chips burning.
It looks like a puddle of blood on your kitchen floor.
It sounds like someone screaming,
Like their best friend has died.
It feels like getting hit in the face with a bat.
It moves fast and quick like a cheetah.
It affects people by making people angry
By tripping them over.

Josh Davies (9)
Benedict Biscop CE Primary School, Moorside

Sunshine

Birds singing like the choir
Dogs running around happily together
Babies laughing on their play mats
Children playing with their water guns
Children sneezing when they smell the pollen
Children laughing when they go down the slide
Ice cream melting in children's hands
The sound of the water swishing side to side
The sound of the adults laughing at a barbecue.

Rebecca Brewis (8)
Benedict Biscop CE Primary School, Moorside

Rain

Dogs huddled in their kennels.
Children crying because they can't get out to play.
Rain pelting off cars like bullets.
Children putting on coats to go out to play.
Car lights reflecting off water on the road.
Cats screaming like little children in the wet rain.

Christopher Simpson (8)
Benedict Biscop CE Primary School, Moorside

Sunshine

The sun shines
As people go racing out
Bangs of garage doors
Sunbeds come out dirty and dusty
Children splashing into
Pools on a hot summer's day
The flow of rivers again and again
Gardeners planting
But the sun is still shining.

Kirsten Baillie (8)
Benedict Biscop CE Primary School, Moorside

Sunshine

The morning sun will come out high
Birds flying in the air like kites
People start to come outside
Children have started playing
On their bikes and in their pools
Later on they are at the beach -
It is full of hot children
And the tickle of ice cream rolling down your fingers
At the end of the day sunburn will be shown
So we splodge on some suncream
At the time when the sun will fall
We will go to sleep and wait for another fun day.

Melissa Campbell (8)
Benedict Biscop CE Primary School, Moorside

Sunshine

Sunshine cracking through the white fluffy clouds
Children playing
And eating ice cream
People playing with each other
Sharing toys to be kind.

Adam Borthwick (9)
Benedict Biscop CE Primary School, Moorside

Thunder

Moaning mams can't get their washing out
Hot chocolate pouring out of the spout
Baby birds sit with their mams
When the thunder *booms* and *bangs*
Everybody cries and cries but the thunder only get worse
And that's how bad thunder is!

Hannah Vincent (8)
Benedict Biscop CE Primary School, Moorside

Snow

Children and parents sledging up and down hills
Angry people kicking their cars
It sounds like ping-pong balls falling from the sky
Crushed carrots on the ground
Hot chocolate bubbling on the oven
Snowflakes falling to the ground like little angels
People wrapped up in their warm clothes
It's dark and everyone is in.

Abbie Atkinson (8)
Benedict Biscop CE Primary School, Moorside

Sunshine

Ice cream melting in children's hands
The laughter of children playing
Birds singing their wonderful songs
Babies laughing as they play on their play mats
The sound of swishing water in the paddling pool
The laughing adults at a barbecue
The sound of children screaming as they go down a slide
The sound of bikes on the grass
End of the day, everybody in.

Megan Thornton (8)
Benedict Biscop CE Primary School, Moorside

Wind

Bird feathers falling to the ground like thousands of leaves
Kites battling in the air like samurai warriors
Leaves hitting each other like dodgem cars
Dogs' fur blowing about like a windmill.

Callum Wilson (8)
Benedict Biscop CE Primary School, Moorside

Thunder

Boom, bash, crash
The wind howling
Scared babies are crying
Children's faces in candlelit windows
Horrified dogs howling and barking like they're mad
The taste of hot chocolate running down my throat
The storm has stopped
And look outside, a rainbow!

Millie O'Brien-Bird (8)
Benedict Biscop CE Primary School, Moorside

Fog

Fog is blurry,
Cold,
You could crash and bash
Like you can't see,
You have to be careful,
Steamy.

Jack Briggs (7)
Benedict Biscop CE Primary School, Moorside

Sun

Steaming warm
Like a fireball,
Burning, turning,
Gassing,
Hot,
Dangerous.

Miles Fortune (7)
Benedict Biscop CE Primary School, Moorside

Snow

Snowballs hitting children on red noses
Angry bus drivers as teenagers lash snowballs
Like cannonballs at the buses
Sledges zoom down white hill like a bullet
Almost knocking over an old lady
Children crying with *iced* up wellies.

Matthew Clark (8)
Benedict Biscop CE Primary School, Moorside

Wind

The wind is blowing the leaves
Like a tornado destroying houses
Children screaming while flying kites
An old woman chasing hats
People falling over
The wind has stopped, time to go in.

Dominic Naylor (8)
Benedict Biscop CE Primary School, Moorside

Scary Storms

It's cloudy
And windy
Grey and black sky
Cars having crashes
It's freezing
And rainy
It sounds like
A big drum
Thunder crashing and bashing.

Rebecca Dagg (8)
Benedict Biscop CE Primary School, Moorside

Fog!

Twirling, whirling around the windscreen,
Steams up the windows,
Everyone screams!
Like being in a giant smoke cloud,
No one knows when it's coming!
No one knows where they're going!

Madeline Squires (7)
Benedict Biscop CE Primary School, Moorside

Snow

Lovely white and brown,
All muddy and messy,
All of it freezing,
Some of it cold,
But it is bold.
When snowballs whizz
I can never avoid them.
When I eat it
I have to have hot chocolate
To warm me up!

Bradley Logan (7)
Benedict Biscop CE Primary School, Moorside

Storms

Scary storms!
Be wary,
It's scary.
Bang!
Clang!
Dogs barking like mad.
Whirlwind!
'Argh!'

Beth Defty (8)
Benedict Biscop CE Primary School, Moorside

Storms

Storms go *bang, crack, smash.*
Bounding rainstorms,
Crashing rain splashing off the ground
Like streams of yellow milk pouring on the ground.
Lightning cracking in the sky
All through the night.

Matthew Potts (8)
Benedict Biscop CE Primary School, Moorside

Storm

The storm is a powerful light
In the sky
Shining so bright
Like a zigzag.
Shining so bright
Like a bottle of milk
Squirting across the sky.

James Common (7)
Benedict Biscop CE Primary School, Moorside

Sun

Steam
Hot
Burning
Big
Yellow
Lollipop
Bad
Fire
Steam.

Callum Robinson (7)
Benedict Biscop CE Primary School, Moorside

Thunderstorms

Trees tumble down to the ground
Children and adults cry like babies
Wind roaring like a bear
Cats running like mice
Babies screaming like birds squealing
Candles light a gloomy house
Bears roaring really loud
Babies cry like it is something major
Suddenly stops!

Faye Wright (8)
Benedict Biscop CE Primary School, Moorside

Sun

Sun is great fun
Must put suncream on
Blazing sun
Gives you sunburn
Orange sun
Red skin!

Rebecca Irwing (7)
Benedict Biscop CE Primary School, Moorside

Snow

Shining like salt
Covering my garden
You can make snowmen
People throw snowballs
Cold
Bold
Running down my neck
Like a river.

Katie Innes (7)
Benedict Biscop CE Primary School, Moorside

Horrid Storm!

Frightening
Lightning
In the air
Makes you stare and stare and stare.
It makes a thundering sound
That people don't like.
Hide under the covers
The lightning is out, shiny as a light bulb.

Stephen James Clark (7)
Benedict Biscop CE Primary School, Moorside

Snow

White and brown,
Soft, crunchy and cool,
Covering houses
They look like snow houses!
Covering the ground,
It's like white paint!

Brian Terry (7)
Benedict Biscop CE Primary School, Moorside

Sun

Sun everywhere
Like a huge lollipop,
Sometimes in the air,
Flying like a heating ball,
Making us all go hot
Like a pot of sweetcorn.

Sam Quinn (7)
Benedict Biscop CE Primary School, Moorside

Storm

Lightning like yellow string
Hurts your ears
Deafeningly loud
Makes a cracking sound
It clashes every second
It comes and goes very, very fast.

Dominic Robertson (7)
Benedict Biscop CE Primary School, Moorside

Snow!

Munchy, crunchy snow falling to the ground,
Throwing while it's snowing
And having a good time.
It's just like candyfloss,
Like polar bears crunched up in the air.
It looks like white fur balls,
Like scrumpled up paper.
The snow is gleaming.

Jennie Walton (7)
Benedict Biscop CE Primary School, Moorside

Sun

A tall ball of gas,
It is bright and light.
Moves slowly across the sky
Like a snail.

Lewis Hodgkinson (7)
Benedict Biscop CE Primary School, Moorside

Snow

Crushed carrots lying on the ground
Snowflakes floating to the ground like little baby angels
Snowballs zooming through the air like cannonballs
Icicles stuck on roofs like daggers
Men in Santa costumes chasing after fluffy fake beards
Bright red buses being pelted with snow
Angry men kicking their car because it won't start
Bubbling hot chocolate running down your chin
The smell of hot Christmas pudding tickling your nostrils
The snow settles, it's time for bed.

Matthew Rankcom (9)
Benedict Biscop CE Primary School, Moorside

Sunshine

Pools rapidly losing water
Men and women gardening happily
Children playing in the sun
Barbecue taste in the evening
Mums lying in the sun
The sea scent in the air
Dark comes - everyone in!

Tom Knight (8)
Benedict Biscop CE Primary School, Moorside

Rain

Children howling like wolves because they can't get out to play,
People warming up next to the fireplace today,
The rain making pitter-patter noises on the roof,
Babies waking up in the night saying, 'Boo hoo!'
Gardens getting watered and gardeners shouting, 'Woo hoo!'
Eventually the rain's stopped! And there's a rainbow too!

Thomas Miller (8)
Benedict Biscop CE Primary School, Moorside

My Senses

When I climb a tree
I can feel the wind blowing around me,
I am scared, I nearly fell off the tree.

I can see a flock of birds flapping their wings
In the bright blue summer sky.

I can smell the cut grass
When the lawnmowers have been out.

I can taste the very, very hot food
That my dad just made.

Alex Walker (7)
Cambois First School, Blyth

My Senses

I can feel the wind pushing against me.
It feels so extraordinary.
Can you see the birds flapping their wings?
I can smell salt and vinegar on my fish and chips.
I don't like the taste of peas running down my throat.
I dislike the feeling of someone bullying me
And jumping out at me.

Katie Robinson (9)
Cambois First School, Blyth

My Quad

My quad is good fun.
I like the sound of the rattling engine.
I can see the grey smoke blast out.
I can smell the heavy smell of petrol.
I can taste the lovely Sunday dinner,
Ready for when my quad ride is done.

Alice Smith (7)
Cambois First School, Blyth

With My Eyes

With my eyes
I can see my brother flying up the wing
on the muddy football field.
I can see his face
screwed up thinking, *will I score?*
With my ears I can hear the thunder
crashing around me, warning me
that a storm is coming.
With my nose I can smell the chocolate cake
my nana is baking for me, to eat, yummy.
With my skin I can feel the fierce heat
of the sun upon my skin
and a tiny spider crawling along my chin.

Shane Gray (7)
Cambois First School, Blyth

My Senses

I can feel the sand in-between my dry fingers
trickling through, not able to catch a single grain.

I can see a boat floating in the distant horizon
not connected to the land.

I hear the whoosh of the sea smashing against the rocks,
trying to reshape their harsh outline.

I taste the salt in the sea air
reminding me the sea reaches out past its edges.

I smell the fresh scent of the salty air.
The smell brings me memories of my holidays in Scotland.

Jordan Campbell (8)
Cambois First School, Blyth

My Motorbike

On my motorbike I use all my senses.

I use my amazing sight to see where I am going,
to see what is around
to keep my eye on the ground.

I can feel the untamed wind blowing against me,
I have to hold on tight,
hold on with all my might.

I can hear the engine revving
and tearing up the grass.
As I speed out on my motorbike
I wonder if anyone can hear me,
and its throaty roar shouting out.

Before I ride I need to fuel the monster,
to refill its energy.
I hold my nose at the strange odour,
it makes me feel unwell.

I have had a long day, I'm covered in thick mud,
I can't wait until I get home
to taste my dad's Yorkshire pud!

Grant Walker (9)
Cambois First School, Blyth

My Dad's Boat

The roar of my dad's boat makes my ears throb,
The sound chugs through my feet.
If I stare at the sea my tummy feels seasick.
I can smell the heavy smell of petrol catching the back
of my throat.
It's good to be out, feel the salty sea spray
Across our faces, the moving of the seagulls
Calling time to return to taste Sunday dinner,
Tie up the boat, check on our catch,
Boat bobbing, waiting for the next time.

Carl Calumboski (8)
Cambois First School, Blyth

My Pets

I have a dog,
A dog called Lilly,
Bouncy, jumpy, waggy tail,
Eight o'clock walks.

I have two turtles,
Green and flat,
Push up on their rock,
Looking out of the tank,
What do they see?

I have a shark,
Grey and sleek,
Torpedo in the water,
Not for stroking,
Not for walking,
Not for touching,
My fingers I like!

Rhiannon Carr (8)
Cambois First School, Blyth

Five Little Senses

I can hear a big, black, gloomy bird
Flying over the blue sea.
I can hear a horse eating the grass
And running around the frosty field.
I can see a dog running for a chewy dog bone.
I can see a sheep sniffing the fresh green grass.
I can smell my dad's yummy Yorkshire pud in the oven.
I can smell my dad's coffee when he puts it in the coffee maker.
I can feel my bed when I go to sleep.
I can feel the table when I am eating my dinner.
I can taste my food for my dinner.
I can taste my food for my supper.

Lewis Gray (8)
Cambois First School, Blyth

Hatred On A Rampage In The Town

All the people hide away,
Hatred is getting closer,
Then he hits someone in the nose.

In the shop he loses it,
He starts to get aggressive
And runs away with a rugby kit.

Hatred approaches a wrestling ring
Where a player cries out in pain.

Then he sees his worst enemy, Kindness!
But no one bets a penny on him.

So the fight was on, the pain dug in,
Unfortunately he got his butt kicked in!

Andrew MacKnight (10)
John F Kennedy Primary School, Washington

Happiness Goes To School

One morning Happiness went to school
in a very bad mood.

Happiness bumped into Hate
and pushed him over and there he lay.

Happiness bumped into Shyness
and Shyness said, 'Come over here and play.'

Happiness bumped into Anger.
'Give me your lunch money,'
'No!'
'Oh you will pay.'

Happiness bumped into sadness.
'Why are you so down today?'

Christopher Leybourne (10)
John F Kennedy Primary School, Washington

Sadness

Sadness clinging on to the door,
doesn't want to let go of the handle.

Sadness shaking, drifting
closer and closer to the house.

Sadness crying, he feels a streak of foolishness
going through him.

Sadness spots Laughter and asks a question,
Laughter mumbles back.

'Oh Sadness you're as quiet as a mouse,'
Sadness says quickly as Fun runs past.
Sadness gets up in the middle of the room.

Sadness has changed,
Sadness is now happy but will he remain?

Francesca Hall (10)
John F Kennedy Primary School, Washington

Laughter

Laughter tickles softly like feathers
But I laugh so hard my side hurts
And sends shivers down my spine

Laughter creeps and tells a joke
I laughed so hard as it fell from my throat
My feet shuffle to Laughter's sounds

As Laughter died I fell asleep.

Francesca Cotton (10)
John F Kennedy Primary School, Washington

Young Writers - A Pocketful Of Rhyme Verses From The North

Fear

Fear is a problem if you are alone
in the house and you see someone hiding.

Fear is a problem if you are shaking
and thinking about the fear that you have.

Fear is a problem if you are scared stiff
and can't move.

Fear is a problem if you are squealing
and moaning and screaming.

Fear.

Jack Short (10)
John F Kennedy Primary School, Washington

Anger

Anger was hurting Fear
and hit him with his fist
And kneed him too.

So Anger got really mad.
He kicked him
really hard and violently.

Bravery stopped Anger
from punching and kicking Fear.

Anger felt overjoyed about stopping
so he turned into Happiness.

Daniel Hylands (11)
John F Kennedy Primary School, Washington

Laughter

Arms quickly flopping while tripping over to the corner
To meet the gang of friends, who will make Laughter welcome.
Legs slowly bending while tumbling over to talk to the gang of friends.
Back, small and bent with scrunched up shoulders,
Shaking while tickling people,
A head wiggling slowly and heavily like a turtle in a race,
A chubby tummy twitching while trying to read a book.

Rebecca Hoseason (10)
John F Kennedy Primary School, Washington

Sunshine

Sunshine relaxes on the bench,
It stretches and closes its eyes,
The glow and heat from its beams
Feels warm and soothing.

How hot is it?

Sunshine drinks in a long cool shower of rain,
A rainbow appears, smiling,
Guarding its pot of gold.

Amy Williamson (10)
John F Kennedy Primary School, Washington

Laughter

Splattered body, shaking
Eggy face bubbling
Long legs wriggling
And long arms squirming
Mouth wriggling like a worm
And ugly body wobbling
Laughter shot past everyone
Just waiting to be seen.

Callum Rutter (10)
John F Kennedy Primary School, Washington

Laughter

Arms wiggling quickly as it
moves towards the group of friends.
Smart shoulders, rolled with its back twisting.
Long legs bending and wriggling them around.
Tummy moving and flopping about everywhere quickly.
Head bobbing up and down very fast
as if it is going to fall off.

Kate Robson (10)
John F Kennedy Primary School, Washington

Hate

Strong arms, held tightly.
Feet stomped, quickly.
Screwed up face, red, angry.
Young and glaring,
Shouting, uproariously at you.
Eyebrows raised, glaring at you,
Hate pushes people aside,
Shouting as it passes.
Hate has no friends.

Rebecca Eleanor Oliver (10)
John F Kennedy Primary School, Washington

Fun

Hands, clapping fast,
Fun's swaying back is swivelling.
Talking loud, Fun's mouth yaps on,
Fun's movement and dance
Brings the day to an end,
But he runs home fast
Wishing tomorrow was now!

Jack Spalding (10)
John F Kennedy Primary School, Washington

Hate

Hate storms past, pushing people aside,
Her arms folded tightly,
Her eyebrows are lined crossly,
Hate runs through her veins.
Her blue eyes roll dramatically
At a circle of happy children,
She flicks her brown hair back confidently
And strides towards them,
Hate's red lips pursue finely,
Her strong legs crossed hard.
She pushes and elbows her way through, yelling:
'Get lost, losers!'
The atmosphere is bitter.
She is Hate.
She burns off her energy, then walks away.

Charlotte Jane Casey (10)
John F Kennedy Primary School, Washington

Hate

Hate storms through the door
Pushing people aside
Shouting, as it turns bright purple
With evil eyes Hate clenches his fists
Harder and harder
Standing tall, Hate pushes over a table
Hate's sharp daggers race across the room
Making people stop and stare
Making sure that anyone and anything
Stays away.

Alexandra Heather Mitchell (10)
John F Kennedy Primary School, Washington

Hate

Hate standing, staring at a group of friends.
She walks over,
Her arms stretched out strongly and pushes them over.
Her confidently crossed eyebrows.
The breezy wind in her hair.
Her red face, burning with hatred.
Her dark blue eyes rolling.
Her ruby-red lips tightly closed.
Her strong legs standing firm.
Then she walks away
With no trace of regret.

Sophie Henderson (10)
John F Kennedy Primary School, Washington

Anger

He has muscle lines all over his arms.
He has very minging teeth.
Legs stiff and dirty.
Head hurting and rough.
Twitchy big blue eyes.
Teeth grinding, dirty, angry.

Daryl McMahon (10)
John F Kennedy Primary School, Washington

Anger

Anger has a super, rare helmet
His muscles bashing in noses
Anger's legs, proudly marching
The speed of his house is incredible
Anger gets on his saddle
And rides into the dark secret night.

Kyle Taylor (11)
John F Kennedy Primary School, Washington

Laughter

Here dives laughter
Crunching and jumping into the waves.
Wobbly arms, joyfully punched
Up into the sky.
Whacked legs, flopping and stretched
Like a banana,
Glary eyes, spied excitingly,
Head berserkly spinning
To the end of the race!

James Wilson (10)
John F Kennedy Primary School, Washington

Fire

The bright fire stings your eyes.
The fire twists and turns.
It flickers in the night.
Fire says, 'Stay away.'
Fire should be watched, not touched.

Loren Toni Fernyhough (10)
John F Kennedy Primary School, Washington

Trouble

Trouble gets you angry
Trouble gets you in a fight
Trouble makes you sad

Trouble steals stuff
Trouble strangles people
Trouble hits you in the face
Trouble kicks you
Trouble bullies you.

Yasmin Corrigan (10)
John F Kennedy Primary School, Washington

Fun!

Fun races past, laughing as the day begins
Legs tight, tense and angry
Arms waving happily
Fun dances and has a laugh and tickles too
Fun moves quickly
Noisy sound, vibrating loudly
Open-wide, curious eyes
Hips moving side to side
Hands clenched and shaking
Fun has joy as it goes home.

Courtney Spencer (10)
John F Kennedy Primary School, Washington

Hate

Eyebrows clenched
Strong like two bow and arrows
As Hate lights a fire
She grins
Quickly walking
She does her evil work
Straight arms like a line
One was dragged away
One was pushed back.

Ben Robson (10)
John F Kennedy Primary School, Washington

Anger

Back straight like a ruler
Fast movement like a cheetah
Thick arms clinging
Giant muscles stretching
His brow crumpled
Completely robust.

William Edward Brightman (10)
John F Kennedy Primary School, Washington

Hate

Staring eyes, rolling red
Strong arms held tightly
Hate drags your old friends away

Hate shouts as people push you around
Hate shouts in uproar
Hate storms over quickly
Pushing as he passes

Until the end of the day
When we all go home
Hoping Hate calms down.

Courtney Barnetson (10)
John F Kennedy Primary School, Washington

The Storm

The storm raged through the door,
The storm shouted in the night.
The storm blew over the table in the garden,
The storm tossed knives everywhere.

Jordan Watts (10)
John F Kennedy Primary School, Washington

The Bonfire

The bonfire twists and turns
The flames lick high into the sky
The fire crackles into the night sky
The flames flicker in the sky
The flames blind onlookers
They are hot and scary.

Brandon Harkess (10)
John F Kennedy Primary School, Washington

Fun

Arms moving around and bending quickly.
Laughing mouth smiling happily and joyfully.
Quickly and loudly laughing sounds.
Bending back jumping.
Head moving back and forward
Dancing and nodding to the sound.
Hands loose, clenched and bent.
Then the fun goes home for more tomorrow.

Sophie Danskin (11)
John F Kennedy Primary School, Washington

Smoke

Smoke blows through the tree.
Smoke walks past the windows of houses.
Smoke plays in the day and at night.
In the morning Smoke is everywhere.
Smoke runs everywhere all day.
Smoke blows out of car exhausts.

Gavin Milroy (10)
John F Kennedy Primary School, Washington

Laughter

Laughter opens birthday present.
Laughter blows out the birthday candles.
Laughter is funny poetry.
Laughter is making funny jokes.
Laughter is sitting next to me.
Laughter is working at school.

Sarah Sweeney (10)
John F Kennedy Primary School, Washington

Heartbeats

Love walked nervously towards the object of his dreams,
Her smile was breathtaking.
As Love drew closer his heart was racing faster.
Happiness was beautiful in every way.
Love's heart was beating like the rhythm of a drum.
She spoke to him.
Love spoke back as hesitatingly as a tortoise.
Happiness was slowly falling in love.
Cloud opened a door and Light shone through,
As blinding as the heat on a summer's day.
Love wrapped his arms tightly around her neck.
His face moved towards her lips.
Their lips touched . . .
Their kiss - blissful.

Charlotte Lesley McIntosh (11)
John F Kennedy Primary School, Washington

Laughter

Laughter giggled cheerfully
and quietly across the road
while shyness went into silent mode
in a shaded corner.

Laughter joyfully encouraged
Shyness into play by saying,
'Dark will be here, before you are here!'

Shyness walked slowly forward
to the metal gate of the park.

Determined to get there before Dark,
he snuck in and sat on the bench.

Laughter crept up and slyly tickled Shyness.
Shyness screamed and laughed and wriggled.

Emma Povey (10)
John F Kennedy Primary School, Washington

Love Struck

Love had met her in the park.
As they walked courage struck!
Like lightning in their hearts.

The further they walked,
the more they saw
of the special thing in their life
they were waiting for.

They came to a sudden halt,
they couldn't help but stare
as they were in love, it wasn't their fault.

Love's heart was beating,
beating as fast as a cheetah,
you could tell he really wanted to meet her.

They slowly kissed, it was heaven,
Love's girl was Happiness,
Love was pure.

Emily Turnock Anderson (10)
John F Kennedy Primary School, Washington

Sea

The sea is angry.
The sea climbs on the lighthouse cleaning the windows.
The rocks and pebbles chatter when they clatter together.
The sea throws pebbles into the sea.
The seaweed tosses and turns in the surf.
We watch the sea race to the sand.
It tickles our toes as we stand.

Stephen Gettings (10)
John F Kennedy Primary School, Washington

Fear Factor

Fear stealthily stealing money -
The alarm was raised,
He was arrested.
He was as scared as a mouse.

Fear doesn't make any friends,
Nobody speaks to him.
Fear is still Fear.

Confidence approached Fear,
They got to know each other really well,
But Fear is still Fear.

Another person approached fear - it was Happy.
Happy told him jokes, he laughed,
But Fear is still fear.

Fun approached Fear, he had a great time -
They played games like dominoes.
Fear thought it was the best,
But Fear is still Fear.

Everyone was playing with Fear,
Doing really good things.
Fear really enjoyed it
And now Fear is Happy.

Dean Farley (10)
John F Kennedy Primary School, Washington

Anger . . .

Face red
Like an erupting volcano

Boiling hot lava
Spewing down the volcano
Like an unstoppable army

Head
Shakes back and forth
Like a raging bull

Aggressive
And loud
Like a giant, stomping, fist in the air

So fierce to others passing by
As he lashes out

Then . . .
One day
When Anger went to spread his fury
Happiness crept up behind him
Wrapping him up

Happiness
Had him in his clutches
Anger . . .
Evolved into . . .
Happiness
Anger was dead.

Craig William Foster (10)
John F Kennedy Primary School, Washington

The Roller Coaster Of Death!

Fear controlled the roller coaster from start to finish.

Fear whispered curses in Sadness' ear.
He tried to fight it, but Sadness couldn't.

It was nearly too late.
Sadness had to fight it, but he was too scared to.

He was as pale as a corpse,
The wind blew his head back, stronger than a giant sneezing.

Sadness couldn't fight it
So the roller coaster got faster and faster.

Until it was too late.
Fear won.
The roller coaster was in a heap of flames, lying there on the floor.
Sadness was gone, never to be seen again.

Anthony Lawson (10)
John F Kennedy Primary School, Washington

I'm Scared!

Fear petrified,
His hair as spiky as thorns,
Sitting as scared as a mouse.

Sitting as nervous as a hunted fox,
Yelling, shouting and squealing.

Away he goes,
Fear screaming,
His mouth wide open.

Shaking like a wet dog,
The ride begins to stop,
Fear is glad.

Fear, running as fast as a cheetah,
Never to return
Again.

Adam Docherty
John F Kennedy Primary School, Washington

The Funfair

There's fun at the fair
What to go on?
The roller coaster or the waltzer
He got off the waltzer
That was fun but
All of a sudden
Fun was sick
In the queue, waiting for the ride
Fun was shivering
Like an ice cube in the freezer

Off he came
Near the end of the night
Fun got a candyfloss
To round the night off
That was fun
Let's do it again on Saturday.

James Jackson (10)
John F Kennedy Primary School, Washington

Anger Vs Devil

Anger is like a volcano,
Roaring at the Devil,
Waiting for its attack.

The Devil shouts at Anger.
Anger strikes back with attack.

Anger kicks him in his stomach.
Suddenly - *bang!*
The Devil strikes him with his red stick,
As red as hot lava.

Anger hits back with a punch,
Now Anger and the Devil are dead!

Lucy McMahon (10)
John F Kennedy Primary School, Washington

Fun

Sun shone
Fun looked pretty as a picture
As she played on the swing

Fun noticed Shyness
Sitting alone
She went to ask him to play

Fun skipped over to help Shyness
He overcame himself
And suddenly became Courageous

They played happily
Fun and Courageous
Were best friends

Fun cheerfully chatted
To Courageous

Afternoon became evening -
The sun was settling down to sleep
The two friends danced back home.

Faye Chenery (10)
John F Kennedy Primary School, Washington

The Wind!

The dark of night,
The scary fright,
The howling wind,
Took flight for the night.

Opening doorways
Then slamming them shut,
Flying down alleyways,
Taking the short cut!

Blowing at the trees
With a slight morning breeze
Sun comes to fight,
Giving wind a fright!

Sun fighting with pride,
With its gleaming light,
The wind backs off
With an icy bite.

World warm with the sun
On boiling heat,
The pride of the sun,
The wind she has beat!

Emma Boxer (10)
John F Kennedy Primary School, Washington

The Fear Fair

At the fair, Fear stomped to the entrance
And got a ticket. He walked off.
Fear looked for something to do.

Fear went to the swings.
He wanted to scare people
With is wicked tricks.

At the gliding swings, Fear whispered to Fun.
'I hope you don't die.'
His voice was like a snake.

Fun screamed and ran off in the mist.
Fear thought it was funny.

Fear's body slithered away
To find someone else to scare.

But when Fear saw Fun crying
His life flashed before his eyes.
His life changed.

Rachel Williams (10)
John F Kennedy Primary School, Washington

Anger

Anger makes you hurt people
Anger makes you mad
Anger shouts when you break its stuff
Anger hits you when you annoy it
Anger brings fear
Anger bullies you
Anger has no friends
Anger makes people sad
Anger hurts you
Anger is hell.

Brandon Black (10)
John F Kennedy Primary School, Washington

The Sounds Of Silence

Have you heard the clouds
Rush across the sky,
Or the green grass
Grow under your feet?

Have you heard a spider
Spinning its silver web,
Or a rainbow being
Painted across the watery skies?

Have you heard a cat
Prowling in the night,
Or the autumn leaves
Falling to the ground?

Have you heard a fish
Swimming in the sea,
Or timid field mice scuttle
Below your feet?

Have you heard the sky
Changing colour each day,
Or the scarlet sun
Sinking slowly in the night?

No, these are the sounds of silence.

Benjamin Hunter (9)
Red House School, Stockton-on-Tees

Autumn

The beautiful coloured leaves on the trees
That fall to the ground with a breeze,
Then dance and play with the wind.
The smell of smoke in the air
When fireworks light up in the sky,
The shouts of excited children,
These are the signs that autumn is here.

Elliott Gibbons (9)
Red House School, Stockton-on-Tees

The Sounds Of Silence

Can you hear the twinkling stars
Shining in the night sky?
Can you hear the rainbow shining
All around the evening sky?
Can you hear the golden sun
Rising in the morning?
Can you hear the birds swooping
High in the sunlit sky?
Can you hear the green grass
Growing every day?
No, these are the sounds of silence.

Holly Featherstone (9)
Red House School, Stockton-on-Tees

Hallowe'en

Werewolves howling,
Zombies are real,
A bite on your neck,
That you can't feel.

Bats in the sky,
The day turns black,
You find a body,
You must go back.

The vampires have taken over,
The skeletons of the dead have awoken,
The fields are no longer covered in clover,
For now, it's the land of the dead!

You want to go home,
Away from harm,
But you are alone,
There's no going back.

Theron Darlow (9)
Red House School, Stockton-on-Tees

Hallowe'en

Dead-looking skeletons,
A spook in the air,
Vampires approaching,
Will you dare?

Mummies live,
Frankenstein's here,
Who did this?
Is he here?

Zombies out,
They are here,
Is it night?
Oh dear!

I know what it is,
It is what you think,
They're all alive,
And it's Hallowe'en!

Animesh Anand (9)
Red House School, Stockton-on-Tees

Autumn

The noise of fireworks,
A cold wind blowing,
Days getting shorter,
Summer flowers dying;
The smell of smoke from the icy cold houses,
Windows steaming up;
Trees losing leaves,
The crackling of conkers falling,
These are the signs that autumn is here.

Stephen Blease (9)
Red House School, Stockton-on-Tees

Autumn

The rustle of leaves,
The afternoons become dark.
The sun is out much less,
People don't wear their summer dress.
The sky goes grey with the clouds,
Cold wind covers you from head to toe.
Children go out less to play,
Night gets longer day by day.
Stars come out during tea,
Leaves go yellow, brown and gold.
Ponds freeze up
And become icy cold.
These are the signs that autumn is here.

Jacob Darlow (9)
Red House School, Stockton-on-Tees

Autumn

The crunch of leaves under your feet,
The screech and bang of fireworks,
The smell of smoke from the bonfire,
Feeling the night chill,
The cold rain on my head,
Shivering in the chilly wind between summer and winter,
Watching the birds fly away to warm places,
Sneaky squirrels collecting conkers,
These are the signs that autumn is here.

Jessica Bedi (9)
Red House School, Stockton-on-Tees

The Sounds Of Silence

Can you hear the snowflakes falling from the sky?
Can you hear the hedgehogs tiptoeing through the night?
Can you hear the raindrops falling?
Can you hear the swaying of the trees?

Can you hear the butterflies flying in midday?
Can you hear the days passing by?
Can you hear the movement as the Earth revolves?
Can you hear the stars twinkling at night?

Can you hear the grass as it grows beneath your feet?
Can you hear the incense as it burns to make a nice smell?
Can you hear the sun as it shines to give us warmth?
Can you hear the sharks as they eat all the fish?

Can you hear the scarecrow as they scare all the crows?
Can you hear your shadow as it follows your footsteps?
Can you hear the clouds as they float in the air?
Can you hear the stinging nettles when they sting you?
No, these are the sounds of silence.

Katrina Wright (9)
Red House School, Stockton-on-Tees

Autumn

I like conker picking,
The bonfire flickering,
The pumpkins at Hallowe'en.
The brown leaves falling off trees,
In the autumn breeze.
I like playing rugby
And getting very muddy.
The frost is near,
These are the signs that autumn is here.

George Baker (9)
Red House School, Stockton-on-Tees

Autumn

When the nights go short,
And the leaves on the trees start to fall,
From the chestnut tree ever so tall,
We gather up the conkers for our games,
The conkers that we give special names,
Squirrels gather up nuts, swallows migrate,
Storm clouds gather and tortoises hibernate,
And best of all Christmas draws near.
These are the signs that autumn is here.

Alex Stephenson (9)
Red House School, Stockton-on-Tees

Autumn

The swaying of trees.
The crackling of the bonfire.
The strong breeze blowing.
The screams of children.
The squirrels and rabbits preparing for hibernation.
The weather getting colder.
The farmers ploughing the fields for harvest.
These are the signs that autumn is here.

Christine Saltikov (9)
Red House School, Stockton-on-Tees

Autumn

When the leaves turn brown,
When the birds fly south,
When the days get dark,
When it's Hallowe'en,
When trees go bare,
When apples fall from the trees,
When we have Bonfire Night,
These are the signs that autumn is here.

Harry Tomlinson (9)
Red House School, Stockton-on-Tees

The Sounds Of Silence

Have you heard the clouds floating in the air,
Or the hedgehogs tiptoeing through the wavy grass?

Have you heard the sand making a swish
When you walk beside the beach,
Or the mouse nibbling his cheese?

Have you heard the frost painting silver patterns on the windowpane,
Or the flowers growing?

Have you heard the sun gleaming on the trees?

No, these are the sounds of silence!

Nanditha Pradeep (9)
Red House School, Stockton-on-Tees

Autumn

The rustle of leaves orange-red, orange and brown.
The crackle of the bonfire and the bang of the fireworks.
Children running around in super, scary costumes.
The sky filled with birds migrating south.
These are signs that autumn is here.

Robert Morgan (9)
Red House School, Stockton-on-Tees

Autumn

The rustle of leaves,
Red, amber, gold and brown,
Falling like peas from a plate,
Hallowe'en, the children wear
Scary and creepy costumes that
Sometimes make you *scream!*
These are the signs that autumn is here.

Sam James Dixon (9)
Red House School, Stockton-on-Tees

Autumn

The rustle of the leaves,
Tumble from the orange, red, brown and yellow trees.
Children crunching on the leaves,
Having leaf fights in the sunset.
Birds migrating to warm sunny countries,
Animals hibernating, lacking food.
Children running round and round all shouting, 'Trick or treat!'
Skeletons, witches, mummies, ghosts knocking at the door.
Screaming grannies, what a shock!
Fizzing, whizzing Catherine wheels.
A bang and a boom, you know what is here.
A crackle and a sparkle and a dazzling sight lights up the sky.
These are the signs that autumn is here.

Olivia Crewe (9)
Red House School, Stockton-on-Tees

Autumn

The rustle of leaves,
Damp, cold air,
The shivery breeze,
Tickling my neck.
I see leaves whirling, whizzing
And swirling.
Above my head I glance at crows.
I notice children running round
In sly, spooky clothes.
Collecting sweets and scaring other children
Enjoying their tasty treats.
These are the signs that autumn is here.

Scarlett Reeves (9)
Red House School, Stockton-on-Tees

Autumn

The rustle of leaves,
A cold chill,
The wind hitting our faces,
The squealing witches,
The children screaming all night long,
The crackling bonfires,
The smell of fire,
The dazzling stars,
The fresh breeze,
The grey sky,
The juicy grass,
These are the signs that autumn is here.

Samantha Mason (9)
Red House School, Stockton-on-Tees

Autumn

The rustle of leaves,
The crunching feeling on your feet,
As they turn into sunset colours.
Nights get darker,
Animals hibernate,
As the noisy children trick or treat.
The cold nights become warm,
Because the fiery feeling of bonfires keep people warm.
The fireworks sparkle and fizzle,
As the dangerous display goes on.
People start to leave,
The noisiness dies out,
These are the signs that autumn is here.

Erin Fleming (10)
Red House School, Stockton-on-Tees

Autumn

The rustle of leaves
Brown-red sunset, all types of colourful leaves
The crunch of shrivelled old leaves under my feet
Falling lightly from the treetops
Bright colourful explosions on Bonfire Night
Dazzling, sparkling, loud, fantastic fireworks
Fill the moonlit sky with shooting stars
Hallowe'en fills the air with screams and shouts
The children run around in spooky scary costumes
Shouting, 'Trick or treat!'
Adults give them something nice to eat
Dressing up as ghouls, goblins, witches and skeletons
Birds fly south and migrate
Animals hibernate
These are the signs that autumn is here.

Grace Hughes (10)
Red House School, Stockton-on-Tees

Autumn

The rustle of leaves
With red, black, green and grey
The sound of kids laughing and running
With the Hallowe'en masks and sweets
The birds fly away to warm places
Hedgehogs hibernate
Days are cool and misty
These are the signs that autumn is here.

Joe Musgrave (9)
Red House School, Stockton-on-Tees

Autumn

The rustle of leaves,
A chill in the air,
The crunch as you step on top of the leaves.
The sweet smell of corn in the dew
Of the morning rush.
The sparkling of sparklers
Sparkling all around.
The strong, merry wind blowing,
The children running to other's houses.
Witches, mad scientists and ghosts on Hallowe'en.
The sweet smell of chewy sweets
And the sound of whizzing and fizzing of noisy fireworks.
The squealing and screaming of Catherine wheels,
The shouting of people saying, 'Look!' and 'Wow!'
Beautiful colours of the rainbow,
Bright hooting and screaming of the loudest fireworks
I have ever heard.

George Wall (9)
Red House School, Stockton-on-Tees

Autumn

The rustle of the leaves
Orange, red and yellow,
Fluttering in the breeze.
The fun of jumping in their piles
As they dry and decay
And the crispy, cool refreshing air at night,.
The sound of fireworks
Crackling and fizzing from over the hill.
Kids screaming and screeching the words, 'Trick or treat!'
These are the signs that autumn is here.

Megan Brineman (10)
Red House School, Stockton-on-Tees

Autumn

The rustle of the leaves, the glowing pumpkins
scattered around all the gardens.
The colourful evening sunsets.
The screeching fireworks,
the loud sigh of the afternoon winds.

The rustle of leaves, the dark morning wake up calls.
The large golden sun rising from the hills,
the tweets of migrating birds flying above the roofs.

The rustle of leaves, orange, gold and amber,
falling from the trees all around me.
Acorns and conkers falling to the ground,
making a crunching sound.

The rustle of leaves, the crackle of the house fires
being lit as the sun goes down.
Winter duvets being put on my bed.
Hot chocolate for bed instead of ice-cold milk.

These are the signs that autumn is here.

Alexander Plahé (9)
Red House School, Stockton-on-Tees

Autumn!

The rustle of leaves
crackle under my feet
and the sound,
'Trick or treat,' hurts my ears.
The children's suits
waving in the breeze.
The fireworks banging in my ear.
These are the signs that
autumn is here!

Harry Bulmer (9)
Red House School, Stockton-on-Tees

Autumn

The rustle of the leaves.
The warming colours, orange, yellow, brown, red, golden,
Soothing colours.
The crunching of the leaves, shrivelled
And starting to decompose and decay.
The nights start to get darker earlier
And the animals start to hibernate.

The scary costumes flood the shops.
Children scaring people in ghost, devil and skeleton suits,
Their mouths stuffed with creamy caramel and soft chocolate.

Shining bright and deafening fireworks,
Screeching, squealing and screaming.
Whizzing and fizzing of the Catherine wheels.

These are the signs that autumn is here.

Joseph Clarke (9)
Red House School, Stockton-on-Tees

Autumn!

The rustle of leaves sending shivers down my spine.
The ear-splitting bang of a flaming firework.
Fireworks prancing in the sky.
Sparks showering the sky.
A grand night for us but not for Guy Fawkes, Bonfire Night.
Leaves scattering all over the ground.
Magpies are migrating along with the other birds.
Happy, happy, happy hibernation.
A mysterious chill with silence is in the air,
Only to be changed by the words . . . trick or treat.
These are the signs that autumn is . . . *here at last!*

Matthew Birch (9)
Red House School, Stockton-on-Tees

Autumn

The rustle of leaves,
The crunching of the golden, yellow and red leaves,
The sigh of a boring, brown, bare tree standing alone,
The sparkles and the crackles in the sky of Bonfire Night,
The banging and the booming of the Big Ben,
The shouts of children saying, 'Trick or treat?' at your door,
The sight of children wearing crazy and creepy monster costumes
And the smell of delicious sweets
And scaring others.
These are the signs that autumn is here.

Sam Burchett (9)
Red House School, Stockton-on-Tees

Autumn

The rustle of leaves,
Scattering round in the garden,
Dry and golden,
Bonfire Night, nice, bright and colourful,
The excitement in the air of all the sparkly fireworks,
Hallowe'en, children fighting over sweets,
Children screeching, 'Trick or treat?'
Most animals hibernating,
The time of harvest,
Farmers picking their crops,
Nights getting darker,
These are the signs that autumn is here.

Kane Hewson (10)
Red House School, Stockton-on-Tees

Autumn

A rustle of leaves,
The smell of nature,
A call from nowhere,
A splash of damp earth,
The frightful winds,
The crackle of twigs,
The muttering of birds,
These are the signs that autumn is here.

Josef Oliver Reilly (9)
Red House School, Stockton-on-Tees

Autumn

The night draws in,
The wind is restless.
Leaves fall from proud oak trees.
Birds get ready to fly to sunnier homes.
We switch on the central heating
And other nights draw in.
Hallowe'en is nearly upon us.
These are the signs of autumn.

Lewis Robinson (9)
Red House School, Stockton-on-Tees

Darkness

Darkness is black like the sky.
Darkness tastes like Hallowe'en spider sweets.
It smells like fire burning.
Darkness looks like scary ghosts.
It reminds me of knocking at doors at Hallowe'en.
It feels like excitement and fear all at once.

Rachael Burder (8)
St Bega's RC Primary School, Hartlepool

Love

Love is bright red like a rose.
Love sounds quiet
but, floating in the air,
this beautiful thing tastes like something special.

Lonely love is sitting
on a lonely wall,
it feels like it is floating in the air
all around you.
This lonely love
reminds me of someone special.

Kristen Cambridge (10)
St Bega's RC Primary School, Hartlepool

Feelings

Feelings make me happy.
Excited is gold.
Envy is a jealous green.
Love is a relaxing rouge-red.
Impatience is an anxious emotion.
Nutmeg is a greeny-brown.
Gracious gold feels warm and soft.
Silence is sparkly silver.

Feelings are multicoloured.

Phillipa Harrion (11)
St Bega's RC Primary School, Hartlepool

Happiness

Happiness is red
like a flower in the sun.
Happiness sounds like a dove
flowing through the lovely sky.
It tastes like sweets
when they have just been made.
It looks like a sunny day
when the sun is just arising.
It feels like something
that cannot be described.
Happiness reminds me
of the sparkling stars
on a night.

Demi-Leigh Milburn (10)
St Bega's RC Primary School, Hartlepool

Loneliness

Loneliness is as white as a whiteboard,
only very quiet,
not very nice,
empty.
Lots of quiet,
yawn all the time.

It reminds me of my grandad
who walks very slowly
and has no one to help him.

Hayden Lynch (10)
St Bega's RC Primary School, Hartlepool

Darkness

It sounds like a creepy door creaking in the night.
Darkness tastes like mouldy old cheese
with a smell so rotten.
It smells like dead fish in the shops.
It looks like a creepy old graveyard
in the spooky night.
It feels like a rough gravestone
with the wind blowing on a spooky night.
It reminds me of a twisty dark tunnel
in the black night sky.
Darkness is like the colour black
waving in the night sky.

Carl Young (9)
St Bega's RC Primary School, Hartlepool

Angry

I am angry red.
My head is bursting,
It feels like a baby screaming,
It tastes like horrible human flesh,
Looking like a bull charging at you,
My heart is burning up like a fire,
It reminds me of a hurricane swarming in the air.

George Harrison (10)
St Bega's RC Primary School, Hartlepool

Young Writers - A Pocketful Of Rhyme Verses From The North

Feelings

Frightened,
excited,
everybody can feel lonely.
If you're nice
good things will happen
so don't be sad.

Angry
really is depressing.
Everyone can be angry
but it doesn't have to upset you.

Gorgeous you feel,
or hurt.
Only feel hurt when you have to.
Don't just do it
because it upsets you.

Megan Lynch (10)
St Bega's RC Primary School, Hartlepool

Love

It reminds me of being with my friends and family.
It feels like romance and being in Heaven.
It sounds like dreaming in a cloud of love.
What colour is it? Love is red like a love heart.
It looks like a guardian angel.
It smells like love in a romantic restaurant.
It tastes like sushi, lobster and fish.

Robyn Hannon (9)
St Bega's RC Primary School, Hartlepool

Happiness

H orse running through a field with a chestnut coat.
A n apple falling from a tree into a tower of apples.
P ink fish being fried on a Caribbean island.
P ink party popper popping into the air.
I gloo getting made by a happy Eskimo.
N ice fluffy dog in its bed.
E xploding eggs in a microwave.
S ilky clothes on the floor.
S nowy days make me happy.

Dillon Johnson (10)
St Bega's RC Primary School, Hartlepool

Love

Love is red like blood,
Love tastes like a Sunday dinner,
Love smells like sunflowers,
Love looks like a heart,
Love reminds me of kissing,
Love feels sad like people dying,
Love sounds like your heart beating after a run.

Daniel Robinson (9)
St Bega's RC Primary School, Hartlepool

Excitement

Excitement is silver and sparkly,
It sounds like the twinkling of a star,
It tastes sweet and sour,
It looks like the moon from afar,
It feels shaky and sparkly,
It reminds me of a little fairy,
Flying through the night's sky.

Amy Ridden (10)
St Bega's RC Primary School, Hartlepool

Tastes I Like

I like Red Bull, the sweet taste of cherries.
Squashy chocolate mousse squashing in my mouth.
I like the sweet taste of chocolate cake slopping in my mouth
And hot chocolate drink, a good taste in my mouth.
I like warm milk leaving a good taste in my mouth and throat.

Aidan Crawford (7)
St Bega's RC Primary School, Hartlepool

Smells

The smell of soapy Dove on nice soft hands.
The lovely barbecue in my mouth.
The Oust air freshener in your bedroom.
The liquid that smells very fresh.
The perfume that you put on your body.
I love the smell of fresh babies.
The fresh rubbers that you smell.
I love the smell of pages in a book.
I love the smell of fresh plants.
The smell of chocolate, melting creamy cake.

Georgia Rochester (7)
St Bega's RC Primary School, Hartlepool

What Is Black?

Black is the colour of the night, scary and spooky,
Black is the colour of a pencil nib
That you write with all day.
Black is a very dark colour.
Black is the colour of a TV screen
Flashing and dashing all day long
Can you imagine living without it?

Jack Purcell (7)
St Bega's RC Primary School, Hartlepool

Love

Love is red like love hearts,
It comes in many different parts.
It reminds me of happiness and romance
Like love at first sight,
But really don't worry, your date won't bite!
Love looks like a giant love heart and red lipstick,
You can get love cards and it is your pick.
Love tastes like red wine and a romantic dinner,
Taking dates to a restaurant is a winner.
It smells like fresh flowers picked with love,
When you get them you want to fly like a dove.
It feels like being picked up by a love bug,
When your date is finished
Give your date a big hug.
Love looks like a giant love heart and lipstick,
The afters at the restaurant
Is good enough to lick.

Devyn Olufemi Wood (9)
St Bega's RC Primary School, Hartlepool

School

Me and my friends play about
When we come to school.
We come to school in a uniform
And our teacher is called Miss Laycock
And she loves maths.
At break time me and my friends play about.
And after that one of the teachers
Blows the whistle and we all line up.

Alex Pringle-Arnell (8)
St Bega's RC Primary School, Hartlepool

Love

Love is pink like a rose,
That opened at the beginning of spring.
It sounds like a choir of angels singing on Christmas Day.
It tastes like melted chocolate when you are really sad.
It looks like the prettiest thing you can imagine.
It feels like silk from the Queen's robe.
It reminds me of getting presents on Christmas Day.

Lucy Lilley (10)
St Bega's RC Primary School, Hartlepool

Darkness

It sounds scary, owls hooting and mysterious
It's annoying
Darkness tastes like chocolate fountains
As brown as muffins, yummy
It also tastes fresh
When you're warm it cools you down

Darkness smells like water and damp sea
Seaweed and sometimes it's horrible, *yuk!*
Darkness looks like black flashing lights
White stars like sweets, *yum!*
It feels soft, cool and maybe warm.

Darkness reminds me of Hallowe'en
Scary things, scary movies
Graveyards and people popping out of my wardrobe
Darkness is the colour of blackness
White, grey and blue.

Katie Bradley (9)
St Bega's RC Primary School, Hartlepool

I Love The Feel Of Things

I like the feel of smooth and soft sheets
And the feel of soft cushions
But the best feel of all is your bed
When you go to sleep
I like the feel of towels
And the feel of my pets; soft fur
But most of all I like the feel
Of my baby brother's hair.

Bethany Williams (7)
St Bega's RC Primary School, Hartlepool

Love

Love is like sparkly pink,
It sounds like church bells ringing,
Tastes like sweet berries,
But looks like a beautiful dove.
Feels like a soft and gentle puppy
And reminds me of a little kitten.

Emilee Pringle-Arnell (10)
St Bega's RC Primary School, Hartlepool

Fun

It reminds me of joy and happiness.
Joy feels like happiness and crying with laughter.
Fun sounds like fun and kids.
The colour for fun is colourful and blue.
Fun looks like a day with your friends and boys and girls.
Fun smells like birthday cake and balloons.
Fun tastes like ice cream and lollipops.

Benjamin Dignen (8)
St Bega's RC Primary School, Hartlepool

Fun

Fun reminds me of happiness and laughter
It looks like lots of party games like pass the parcel and sweet hunts
Fun smells like sweet sugar candy
Its colour is pink and lilac
It tastes like candyfloss and sweet things
Fun sounds like music and shouting all around.

Atlanta Burgon (9)
St Bega's RC Primary School, Hartlepool

Darkness

Darkness smells like sea, salt and rust.
It tastes like fresh air.
The colour of darkness is black and grey
like twisty tunnels and gloomy caves.
It feels like wind roaring at you with strength.
It reminds me of a spooky night in a mansion.
It sounds like trees swishing in the wind and rain
dropping on a tin house.

Nathaniel Skidmore (8)
St Bega's RC Primary School, Hartlepool

Happiness

Happiness reminds me of being together
with my friends and family.
It feels like fun, smiling and playing.
It sounds like a day at the circus
and a game of footie with my mates.
Happiness is blue like the sky.
It looks like a joke that puts a smile on your face.
It tastes like pizza and McDonald's.

Patrick Burder (10)
St Bega's RC Primary School, Hartlepool

Fun

Fun tastes like a good treat.
Fun smells like perfume and a smelly teddy.
Fun reminds me of when you like
Playing your favourite game.
Fun looks like happy things that happen.
Fun feels like you are in bed.
The colour of fun is like the bright sun.

Caitlin Lister (9)
St Bega's RC Primary School, Hartlepool

Happiness

Happiness sounds like laughter
And is funny too
It looks like fun
And it also reminds you of
Friendship
Happiness smells like joy
Its colour is pink and lilac
It tastes of friends and family.

Evie Robbins (8)
St Bega's RC Primary School, Hartlepool

Darkness

Darkness reminds me of Hallowe'en
On a foggy black night,
Its colour is black and grey like a stormy sea,
It sounds like rain falling on a tin roof
And werewolves howling,
It tastes like frost on a cold day,
It smells like thunder,
It looks like a thick black night sky,
It feels cold and terrifying,
I'm scared!

Emily Pettite (9)
St Bega's RC Primary School, Hartlepool

Happiness

Happiness reminds me of people
having a great time like when all your family
go to the sunny beach on a boiling hot day.
Happiness is lots of different colours like fizzy sweets.
Happiness tastes like chocolate.
Happiness smells like joy and fun.
Happiness sounds like people having a brilliant time.
Happiness looks like having a party on your birthday.
Happiness feels like people have a good time and laughing.

Carl O'Sullivan (9)
St Bega's RC Primary School, Hartlepool